Via Dolorosa
& When Shall We Live?

David Hare was born in Sussex in 1947. His first play, *Slag*, was produced in 1970. A year later he first worked at the National Theatre, beginning one of the longest relationships of any playwright with a contemporary theatre. Between 1978 and 1997, the National produced eleven of his plays. Five of his best-known plays, *Plenty*, *The Secret Rapture*, *Racing Demon*, *Skylight* and *The Judas Kiss* have also been presented on Broadway.

DAVID HARE

Via Dolorosa

&

When Shall We Live?

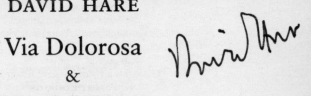

EX LIBRIS

IL MENEGHELLO·MILANO

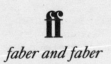

ff

faber and faber

First published in 1998
by Faber and Faber Limited
3 Queen Square London WC1N 3AU

Typeset by Faber and Faber Ltd
Printed in England by Mackays of Chatham plc, Chatham, Kent

A CIP record for this book
is available from the British Library

ISBN 0-571-19752-3

2 4 6 8 10 9 7 5 3 1

Contents

For Nicole,
with all my love

Via Dolorosa

Via Dolorosa was first presented by the Royal Court
Theatre at the Duke of York's on 3 September 1998.

Directed by Stephen Daldry
Designed by Ian MacNeil
Lighting by Rick Fisher
Assistant Director Rufus Norris

Author's Note
The first of my visits to the Middle East was inspired and
organized by Elyse Dodgson from the international
department at the Royal Court Theatre. I owe particular
thanks to Keith Lawrence, Sigal Cohen, Muna Khleifi,
Susannah Pickering, George Ibrahim and Eran Baniel. The
play dramatizes only a very few of the many, many meet-
ings I had. But my special debt is to those who, then and
later, took a personal risk by speaking to me anony-
mously.

Via Dolorosa is a monologue, ideally to be performed by its author. At the outset, the lights go up and the author is found on the stage. He begins to speak.

Author Partly, of course, I just want to see what it's like. That's what I'm doing here. If you're wondering. The last time I acted was when I was fifteen, and played Thomas Cromwell in the school production of *A Man For All Seasons*. Christopher Hampton played Richard Rich and the film critic of the *Financial Times* – as now is – played Thomas More. The experience taught me all I needed to know. Since then, I've always tried to get Judi Dench to do this sort of thing.

And it's a preference, a long-held preference, what you might call a 'habit of mind' – putting words into other people's mouths. And those people are played by people whose profession is to pretend to be other people. For which purpose, they adopt gestures, voices, intonations, even sexual attitudes not their own. On stage, they affect to be ravished and amused by someone whom they will, afterwards, run a mile to avoid having dinner with. Likewise, they spit torrents of abuse against an actor who later, later, in the softness of the night, they will share their bed with. These: the elaborate conventions of theatre, so loved – by me at least – so treasured. So much the very heart of my life.

And yet. Asked to go to Israel, I think 'And what? Go to Israel and *write a play*?'

The girl at Gatwick asks me where I am going. 'Tel Aviv,' I

say and at once she laughs. 'Lucky you,' she says and roars
with laughter. Why? What is she laughing at? Am I missing
something here? What is the joke? What is the joke
exactly?

People always say that in England we lead shallow lives.
Our lives must be shallow because we live in a country
where nobody believes in anything any more. My whole
life, I've been told: 'Western civilization? An old bitch
gone in the teeth.' And so people say, go to Israel. Because
in Israel at least people are fighting. In Israel, they're fighting for something they believe in.

Israel is, first and foremost, a cause; the cause being a
patch of land, north to south on the eastern shore of the
Mediterranean, lying like a small brown anchovy set
down on a school atlas, to which the most persecuted
people of modern times – perhaps the most persecuted
people of all times – after the matchless catastrophe of
the Holocaust rushed in the perfectly reasonable belief
that they would never be safe until they had a country
of their own. 'We appealed to the conscience of the world.
The world has no conscience. We have no one but
ourselves.'

The fight. The struggle. The historic destiny. The return of
the people. The cause: life therefore having a meaning and
shape that eludes the rest of us in the endless wash of
'What the hell are we doing here?' In a single day, says an
Israeli friend, he experiences events and emotions that
would keep a Swede going for a year.

And this tone, my friend's tone, being a tone we will come
to know, a tone we will come to recognize in the next
ninety minutes, a tone, let us say, of necessary dramatiza-
tion: 'We, the Jews. We, the Jewish people. This, the
Jewish homeland.'

4

Zionism itself being a movement with only a short history, and distinguished from other political movements of our time by the fact that it was invented by a playwright. Yes, Theodor Herzl, in 1894 takes a mere three weeks to write his play *Das Neue Ghetto*, in which the Jewish hero, struck down by his enemy, dies at curtain-fall, his last words ringing out through the darkened theatre: 'I want to get out! Out of the ghetto!'

Nine years later, the same Herzl is Chairman of the World Jewish Congress when Lord Lansdowne, on behalf of the magnanimous British Empire, is generous enough to offer a small chunk of Uganda as a suitable place for the Jews to 'live and observe their national customs'. Incredibly, a fair number of delegates are hotly in favour – a bird in the hand is worth two in the bush, and Africa, after all, is better than nothing – but the option is finally rejected on the grounds that Uganda does not have the spiritual quality the Jews require. From this moment on, the central argument is foreshadowed. Is this a Biblical mission? Or is it a secular state?

Like many writers, I am often asked to go. In the early eighties I am asked by an organization called the Friends of Israel. They say they would like to pay for me to go and see their country. I say, sure, I'd be delighted. They say: one condition. They have fixed that on my return I will speak about Israeli culture on the BBC radio programme *Kaleidoscope*. 'But what if I don't like Israeli culture?' Bewildered, they reply, 'But you will like Israeli culture . . .'

Later, my then-friend Philip Roth returns home inspired by his meeting with the settlers, those religious Jews who have turned their whole lives into an act of political defiance by establishing Jewish townships on hitherto Arab land. 'You've got to go, David. You've got to go and see it for yourself. These people are absolute lunatics. They're the maddest people I've ever met in my life. For any writer of fiction, they're the most wonderful material.' 'But surely,' I say to Philip, one of America's most gifted comic novelists, 'they're *your* material, not mine.' 'Oh no,' says Philip. 'You have no idea. These people are so crazy there's room enough for all of us.'

On both occasions I refuse. It is only now, it is only ten years later, that I realize, almost without noticing, that for some time my subject as a playwright has been faith. My subject is belief. And so it comes to seem appropriate – no, more than that, it comes to seem urgent – that the fifty-year-old British playwright should finally visit the fifty-year-old state.

The week before, the Israeli novelist, David Grossman, comes to my house in Hampstead. He tells me that whenever he comes to London he makes sure to walk on Hampstead Heath. 'I have some sort of mineral reaction to the place I don't get anywhere else in the world. Just to breathe the air makes me feel happy.' Obscurely, I feel proud when he says this, as if somehow Grossman's happiness in Hampstead reflects credit on me, as if it were part of the glory of happening to be British to be able, rather casually, to offer foreigners the wonderfulness of Hampstead Heath. But 'mineral reaction'?

Grossman has thought so deeply about Israel and has lived so long with people like me asking questions that he can't help wincing at my clumsiness.

'What you call the major problems of Israel can one day be solved. There will be a Palestinian state. When I said this ten years ago, everyone told me I was crazy. Now in their hearts people know it will happen. There are huge issues. But they are essentially soluble. What is less soluble is the underlying moral question: how does a majority which itself has been historically unloved now deal fairly with an unloved Palestinian minority in their own midst? Are we mature enough, are we courageous enough to internalize the idea of equality?

I say, surely there's a problem at the heart of Zionism. Israel is effectively a religious state. It now admits immigrants of only one faith. Won't it one day have to become a modern country, multicultural, like any other?

Grossman smiles. 'Yes, but for us that's very difficult. I don't see it the way you do. I don't think you have to be religious to be a Jew. There is no God in my life, and I'm as Jewish as it's possible to be. If you want to understand Israel, look to the Six Day War. That war changed everything. Myself, I feel we were much more Jewish before 1967. That war destroyed our essential Jewishness, because up till then places and buildings and stones didn't mean anything to us. They weren't important. What mattered to us were ideas.

'Something very profound happened to Israel during the Six Day War. For the first time we seized land, we took land by conquest and suddenly the religious Jew saw the Bible not as an historical story, but as a contemporary operations manual. Yes, of course, I want Israelis to have access to the Wailing Wall, but I don't need to own it. Nor do I need to own any of these holy places. It's new, this idea. That you have to own things. It's new and it's profoundly un-Jewish.'

People have warned me that Israelis are loud and argumentative. But David Grossman, to the contrary, sits on my white sofa in Hampstead. Just an hour in his thoughtful company makes me realize that my planned visit is laughably incomplete. You cannot visit Israel unless you also visit its twin, its underside. What is the point of going unless you walk through the mirror into the occupied land – even the language is contentious – into what, since the 1993 Oslo Agreement, we have called the Palestinian territory, but which one day – in another people's dream, for this is the Middle East and everyone is dreaming – which one day may be called the state of Palestine?

On arrival in Tel Aviv I am rushed along Californian highways in the company of Sigal Cohen, the young and humorous translator who will accompany me wherever I go. I had expected massive security precautions and I boast to Sigal of the ease with which I have sailed through immigration. 'Yes,' she says. 'Israel is an easy country to get into but it's an impossible country to get out of.'

At my nasty Western-style downtown hotel, my chief host, Keith Lawrence, is waiting. He is very thin, like a Teddy boy with tapered trousers and a collarless jacket. Give him a cappuccino and this could be Old Compton Street. He is the modern face of the British Council. No whiskered old buffer he. He is the man who is bringing stuff like *Shopping and Fucking* to Tel Aviv. He has been here three months and is very excited. He keeps saying Tel Aviv is sexy and a happening kind of place, especially for a beach bunny, and sometimes he talks, rather unexpectedly, about the 'buzz'. We get into a long discussion about mobile phones. I try to find out exactly what the buzz consists of, but everyone tells me it has mostly to do with sitting in cafés and fucking. Someone says to me later that Tel Aviv is the fucking capital of the world.

No chance to observe, because I am off to eat baked sea bream, in a stunning waterside restaurant in the nearby port of Jaffa, with the Israeli theatre director Eran Baniel. Eran is a fine-looking man in his early fifties, bearded, articulate, in a black corduroy suit. Now we drink

Rothschild's Red Merlot and talk about the profound divisions which have emerged in Israel between the secular and religious ways of life.

At the foundation of the state, the religious orthodox were guaranteed a special status. Anyone who entered a yeshiva to study the Talmud was exempted from the army, and given a public salary. At the time there were just 500 students, but by the early 1990s there were over 100,000, says Eran, 'effectively living off the state for life'.

'For years, the Jew believed that when the goy persecuted you, it gave you the right to short-change him. Hence the racial stereotype of the Jew who smiles while he swindles you. Well, now *we* are the goy. Israel is the goy. And the religious orthodox have become the thieving Jew. They go to whoever wants to be Prime Minister and say, yes, you can have our votes but only if you promise to give us our money. They smile and smile, and rob the country blind. They don't serve in the army. They don't work. They do nothing. It's like Chekhov. There are fifty-year-olds who've been so-called studying all their lives.'

Eran, it is clear, is a secular Jew. His life was changed by his famous co-production of *Romeo and Juliet*. This was presented in the middle of Jerusalem. The Palestinians played the Capulets and the Jews played the Montagues. The project took eight years to achieve. There were five months of rehearsal, with the Palestinian producer George Ibrahim in charge of the Capulets and Eran directing the Montagues. The whole experience opened his eyes. Any Palestinian who wanted to see the play in Jerusalem had to be vetted by the Israeli Ministry of Culture, the Prime Minister's Office and the Ministry of Defence. For an Arab, even to see a play became a privilege, not a right.

In this production the Capulets *really* hated the Montagues. It was not a production about love, but about hate. Neither side needed the rhetoric at the beginning. 'You know that bit', says Eran, 'where the two sides line up and sort of say "Fuck you, Montague" and "Fuck you, Capulet". We cut all that. Because Israelis and Palestinians go straight to the emotion: you pick up a stone and throw it straight away.'

From the very start the Palestinians said: 'We're not going to have all that nonsense at the end where the families kiss and make up and say everything's going to be all right.' In the present context, what would that mean? 'Like a stupid Israeli, I took it personally. I was insulted. I said Rabin and Arafat had shaken hands, why couldn't the characters in the play? Of course, it's only when you begin to see yourself as the occupier and them as the occupied – and all that means – that you stop taking things personally, as personal insults.'

Eran says he never really understood the occupation until he did this job. 'Most Israelis don't even notice the Palestinians. They don't see them. Have you seen how Israelis drive? They don't drive. They *own* the road.' His voice is rising now. 'Have you been to the Palestinian territories? Look how the water is allocated. In the settlements, you have the obscene spectacle of Israelis sitting by their swimming-pools while Palestinians carry their drinking water round in jerry cans.' He uses a phrase I have heard before. 'It's un-Jewish, it's un-Jewish behaviour.'

Eran interests me most when he tells me about an actress he worked with who became religious. One day she came to him and said that she'd decided to give up acting because it was wrong. All theatre is wrong, all fiction is wrong. God makes the stories. What right have we to invent new ones?

I have been reading George Steiner who argues that the Jews are not cut out to be artists. The Jewish impulse is to know, not to invent. The world is there to be understood. It is a lifetime's work to try and interpret its complexity. Why fecklessly create new complexity? It is no coincidence that the great scientists and theorists are Jewish – Einstein, Freud, Marx. Yes, there are Jewish storytellers like Kafka, like Proust, but they are the exceptions. As in Talmudic study, the highest good is to work, to learn. For the rest, why rival God? Why fabulate?

By chance, my own modest piece of fabulation, *Amy's View*, is currently rehearsing at the Cameri, one of Israel's foremost theatres, which for some reason is situated in a particularly dismal shopping mall, God knows where, in downtown Tel Aviv. A few days later, Keith Lawrence and I kick our way through the litter-strewn streets. 'It's so odd,' he says. 'They feel so strongly it's their land, but what do they do with it? There's garbage everywhere, they throw plastic bottles out of car windows, they put pylons right across the countryside. Their power stations belch black smoke. They wait two thousand years for the promised land, then all they do is pollute it.'

At rehearsals, all the gossip is about yesterday's Israeli equivalent of the Oscars. Every single acceptance speech was about politics. The Best Actress lamented the assassination of Rabin, while the Best Actor called for the impeachment of the Prime Minister, and told him to go boil his head. The rhetoric so infuriated one right-wing member of the audience that he retaliated with a bomb hoax and everyone had to leave the hall. As the organizer said rather plaintively, 'All the suspense leading up to Best Picture was lost.'

The cast of *Amy's View* have two hours of questions. At one point I say the play is about how we no longer expect society to validate our beliefs. Our only values are private values. The last line of the play is 'So. We're alone.' Israel, I say, may be worst place in the world to perform the play, since here people are still arguing passionately about where their country is heading. Whereas in England Tony Blair represents all things to all men. What does he believe? Nobody knows. What will he do? Whatever is popular. Where is he heading? He never tells us. At once, an Israeli actor interrupts: 'Oh please, please, send us your Tony Blair.'

In fact, theatre is making me impatient because I am longing to get going and spend Sabbath in the Jewish settlement of Sheri Tikva which lies some miles inside the borders of the Palestinian territory. It takes us hours to push our way out of town on a Friday afternoon, in the pre-Sabbath rush, but finally Tel Aviv falls away, and the road opens out. I think of my Sunday school, Sunday afternoons in a stuffy wooden hall in Bexhill-on-Sea. I look from the window of the car and the pale, stony landscape of dusty hills and olive groves feels familiar, like a drawing from memory.

I have now to be careful, because ten minutes later a feeling arrives, unbidden. My mind is slipping, I am dreaming, perhaps of Israeli wine and fresh fish, when suddenly, in open country at last, it occurs to me, as I look out the window, *that the Jews do not belong here*. This feeling is so unexpected and of course implicitly so inflammatory that I turn guiltily, blushing, to see whether anyone in the back of the car can tell what I'm thinking. Up till now I have been in Tel Aviv, a town which, on its surface at least, is sophisticated and Western, and of course I have been enchanted by the actors and producers I have met, but now I am speeding through a huge land mass – I feel the topography, I feel the land, a great hot continent stretching away to my right, Arab country after Arab country – and for the first time I understand how odd, how egregious Israel must look to the Arab eye.

Slightly shaky now, distrusting my own processes, we are approaching the border with the West Bank. I have known for some time that Sigal does not approve of my visit to the settlements. Now as we cross over, she is becoming farouche, shifting in her seat and looking grumpy. 'I wouldn't do this, I wouldn't be coming here if it weren't for you.' And the Israeli driver isn't happy either. 'When I was in the army, we wasted months patrolling these places, protecting people who are only here to make mischief.' 'It's against my principles,' Sigal is saying, but I am riveted by the splendour of the four-lane highway, which cuts across the valley and leads . . . well, nowhere. Only to this one small settlement.

I suppose I had been expecting something pioneering. I had the idea that settlements would be like the Wild West, timber-frame buildings slung up, everything muddy and makeshift. Far from it. To my amazement we are coasting smoothly into an area not unlike Bel Air or Santa Barbara. Nestling in Arab hills is a beautifully landscaped, middle-class community of detached houses, each with its own lawn. The nearest I can get to describing it is to say that, but for the barriers and armed guards, it looks like one of those towns Steven Spielberg uses when he wants to show aliens arriving to disrupt total suburban normality.

As if this is not surprising enough, I am saying goodbye to Sigal – she certainly ain't staying – and shaking hands not with a couple of bearded zealots but with Danny and Sarah Weiss, whose American-type home is littered with Delta timetables and yesterday's copy of the *New York Times*. Sarah is thin, small and open-faced, in her forties; Danny is older, exhausted from travelling around the world as an agent for opera singers. He is thrilled that I am a playwright and plans to spend the Sabbath picking my brains about directors. Is someone called Trevor Nunn any good?

Inside, their children are running around, cheerfully making their last phone calls and setting the timer switches for the lights which must turn on and off automatically once Sabbath begins. I am forbidden to lift my pen in front of them, so I will spend a lot of time in the next couple of days dashing back to my room to make notes. They don't mind as long as they don't see. There is some confusion whether the deadline today is 4.15 or 4.16, but men, unlike women, are anyhow allowed an extra eighteen-minute window to go on doing irreligious things until 4.33. No one can tell me why.

As we walk back after synagogue for the family meal, Danny begins to tell me why they are here. Years ago they tired of America as a place without any spiritual values, and where life is completely empty and meaningless. When they first got here, Danny and Sarah lived in the city. But Sarah decided she wanted to make what she calls a 'contribution', i.e. to live in a disputed place. What they value here, apart from the sense that they are building something, is the natural friendliness of what I learn to call not the 'settlement' but the 'community'. When Sarah went to the States for two weeks, her neighbours insisted on taking in all six of her children. These same children play safely in the street. It's like America before the fall.

At dinner, they are both angry at the frosty reception that Binyamin Netanyahu, Israel's controversial Prime Minister, has just had from American Jews. Americans are furious that he has yielded to the religious orthodox the right to decide who is a Jew. Jews in the US say they loyally support Israel and send it huge sums of money. So what right has some Israeli rabbi to legislate who is and isn't Jewish?

Danny and Sarah are unimpressed by this argument. They are also contemptuous of American support. 'Of course American Jews support Israel. Why wouldn't they? It's simple self-interest. Israel is the insurance policy of the whole Jewish people. So that doesn't impress me at all. No,' says Danny, 'this is an argument about conversion. The Jewish religion is one of the most complex in the world, with the most highly developed system of laws. It isn't enough to say you *want* to be a Jew. It's like joining a country club,' says Danny. 'You can't just walk in.'

This hotly contested subject leads us naturally to the most hotly contested subject of all: what right do people like Danny and Sarah have to be on land stolen by conquest, and how do they answer the charge of deliberate provocation? Danny says it's quite clear. Yes, it's a good thing to build a new country, to build cities. After the Shoah, that in itself is something good. But Israel must have roots as well. It can't just be a bolt-hole. It has to be the place where life goes right down deep into the soil.

God didn't promise the Jews Tel Aviv or Haifa. What he promised them was the land of Judaea and Samaria. The justification is in the Bible. In 1967 the Israeli Prime Minister warned the King of Jordan not to join in any Arab attack, so he only had himself to blame when the Israelis moved eastwards to reclaim Biblical lands. The Israelis did not start the Six Day War. It was forced upon them. It became the greatest victory in Jewish history. His daughter adds quietly, 'No, it was the greatest victory in all history.'

'What's the difference, you asked us,' says Danny, 'between living in Israel and living in the US? I put it like this. Memorial Day here is a day where we all get out of our cars, wherever we are, in the middle of the road and stand for two minutes remembering the dead. In the US it's a day when you have a mattress sale. Memorial Day Sale! Mattresses cheap! That's all it means. Here, whether you were secular or religious, you wept that day when the Biblical land was returned.'

I say it seems anomalous that in the heart of Palestinian territory there should be an enclave in Hebron where 521 Jewish militants have to be protected by four thousand Israeli troops. It's a farce. Danny disagrees. Hebron is one of the two most holy Jewish places because it is the first piece of land that Abraham bought. The very first commercial transaction a Jew ever made was when Abraham bought Hebron for two hundred shekels. And the deal, says Danny, *has never been rescinded.*

Further, it was in Jerusalem, on the Mount of the Rock, that Abraham was prepared to offer his son Isaac as a sacrifice to God. It was David who bought Jerusalem – the price is now checked and found to be four hundred shekels, again, says Danny, hitting the table with his finger, a watertight transaction, recorded and still legal – and Solomon who built the First Temple there. The Abyssinians destroyed it. Herod built another and the Romans destroyed that. The ultimate purpose of Jewish life is to build the Third Temple, which will follow the redemption of the Jews and prefigure the coming of the Messiah. One day the Arab mosques which currently stand on the rock will be gone and the Third Temple will rise in their place.

All of this is pleasant enough – we are eating and drinking contentedly – but things take a more combative turn with the arrival of their Canadian neighbour, Miriam. At once the temperature rises. Miriam was one of the first settlers in the pioneering days. In the eighties, she says, you could shop freely in Arab towns, but then the Palestinian uprising, the *intifada*, destroyed all that. Later, Miriam had moved back to Tel Aviv but, in her words, 'When they signed the Oslo Accord, I thought, here we go again' and defiantly she decided to do her bit by moving back into a settlement.

For these people, Oslo, the first ever peace accord between Palestinians and Jews, is the great betrayal. And the man who signed it – Yitzhak Rabin, who was later gunned down by a Jewish religious fanatic – is of course the great betrayer. 'He was once Minister of Defence but I never noticed he did much defending,' says Sarah. 'Worse than that,' says Miriam, 'we are only now beginning to know the truth about Rabin's assassination.' It turns out, she says, that Rabin knew in advance that he was going to be assassinated. And he did nothing about it. 'Hey, why didn't he just buy himself a cross and put himself on it?'

When Miriam has gone, Sarah offers to take me for a walk through the deserted streets. It's a dark night, and in the distance you can see lights from the ramshackle Arab villages and hear the tinny music drifting across. Sarah gestures towards her own prosperous surroundings. 'The whole world is telling us: Freeze! Freeze the settlements! I say: telling someone to freeze is the same as telling them to die.'

I ask if it's true that yuppies are trying to avoid going into the army. 'Oh no, it's not really true. I've read stories about it in the papers. The real point is that people are tired. The war has been going on for so long. It's very hard for people from outside to understand what toll that takes on you, always living in fear, always knowing people who've lost sons and daughters, brothers and sisters.

'We have to be here. It's incredibly important we're here because we know from history that unless we stay here we have no chance at all. I'm not just talking about the Holocaust. At every point in Jewish history you will find that whenever they thought there was a moment of safety, persecution started again. It makes me laugh when America says it's our ally. Oh yes? And just how long would it take you to get here? No, no, no, it's us and no one else. Look, there's an Arab village over there, and I want them to be able to live here alongside us. I'd like it to be possible. But I don't know. There's a fine line of distrust.'

I ask her what she means. There is a silence. Then: 'At bottom, I think they want to kill us.'

We are silent now as we walk further down the neat, perfumed streets, the stars bright above us, and the lights of the Arab villages a subtly nicotine yellow. Up till now I have only been swimming in the coral reef of these arguments, noticing something interesting here, picking out a sudden flash of colour over there. But now with Sarah, I am out to sea, in the depths of the thing, and my feet no longer touch the bottom.

I say that this is incredibly depressing, and at the same time contradictory. On the one hand, Sarah is telling me that the Jews have to be here. On the other hand, she says they are surrounded by people who will always want to kill them. What is the way forward? 'Not pieces of paper called Oslo.' 'No, I know what you think the way forward *isn't*. I am asking what the way forward is.' 'I look at my children and I want them to live in a peace I haven't had.' 'But how is it to come?' 'I don't know.'

More walking, more silence, this time gloomier.

'The Lord promised us the Land, but he never promised it was going to be easy. You don't come to Israel if you think it's going to be easy. You may not be religious, but actually you need deep reserves of faith. We appear to be more divided than at any time in our history, but deep down, the secular people respect the religious people. If the moment came, we'd all be united again.'

This speech moves me, and I like Sarah. But I'd like her more if she didn't now go on to tell me that Peres was way off line, the Labour Party was corrupt, and Ben Gurion was a communist. And a worse thing happens when we get home. She asks me if I'm married and have children. I explain that my wife is Jewish. Her family fled from Turkey. Her mother and father hid from the Nazis for a year in a barn in France. My wife has taken the exact opposite course to their own. Not only has she married a Gentile, but one cousin has married a black man. Another cousin lives with an Arab. 'And what's funny is the Jewish family's fine about it,' I say, laughing. 'It's the Arab girl who doesn't dare tell hers!'

I feel Sarah withdraw from me. Up till this, I have been an observer. Now I am the husband of an assimilationist. 'So what you're saying is there won't be any Jews in the next generation,' she says. 'Tell your wife, maybe she feels accepted. But tell her to remember: to be accepted, you don't have to be the same.'

I've reached a low point, it's obvious, and next morning I'm not crazy to get up from my bedroom with its bomb-proof steel door to resume what seems to me a subtly insane dialogue. Nothing wrong with the philosophy This Is How We Want to Live, so long as you don't attach the lethal dangler: This Is How We Want To Live, So Fuck You.

But luckily my mood is not infectious, because at noon we are bowling downhill to spend time with Miriam's family who are already ranged round the kitchen table eating a delicious-looking stew. Sadly, we cannot sample it, because today they are eating meat and we have been eating dairy. If we were German, we might be able to, because Germans need only three hours to switch from one to another, and the Dutch are allowed to let just one hour pass. But our ways are those of Eastern Europe where six hours have to go by, so instead we just drink and talk and everything is fine.

Various American Presidents are discussed, including Nixon, who, they say, was not a good person 'but he saved Israel's ass, so he's fine by me'. Danny explains that although Nixon called Kissinger the Jew-boy and spoke of people as kikes, he was not a real anti-Semite, because he was equally rude about all races, like Ities and Micks. 'He was anti-Semitic but he wasn't really.' Bush comes in for particular opprobrium for not finishing off Saddam Hussein; Reagan was an actor; and Carter was a disaster.

Everyone wants to know what I'm doing here, and by way of explanation I say I've got a play at the Cameri. 'Oh theatre! Theatre! Well, you must know some very left-wing people.' The news that I am scheduled to meet Menachem Begin's famous son, Benni, leads us back to the subject of Rabin and his wife Leah ('Ugly, a very ugly woman to look at,' says someone, getting in an early blow) and what he knew of his own assassination. Suddenly, the atmosphere turns quite nasty. Miriam's elderly husband, Ron, is shouting that everyone knows that the assassin was put up to it by a government *agent provocateur*. The whole assassination was a plot to discredit the right wing and the settlers. Sarah becomes equally voluble. 'Ron, Ron, you don't have to twist the facts. I happen to agree with your theory, but it isn't yet proved.' But Ron is now raving about how you can't trust anybody, there are agents everywhere, so Danny tactfully suggests we leave. In the street afterwards Danny tells his wife to calm down. 'Just be calm when you talk.' 'I am calm. I am perfectly calm!'

But I have learnt something important. Nothing unsettles the settlers more than the idea that Rabin's death is their fault. The murder of a Jewish leader by a Jew travesties the very meaning of their existence. But no two settlers have the same strategy for refuting it. So they pick away, deconstructing the event with the same textual vigour that they bring to the Talmud.

First person: Netanyahu can't have known the security double agent was going to be in the crowd that day because the official report tells us . . . Next person: Yes, but the official report was itself drafted by elements friendly to . . . and so on.

Meanwhile, at my side, Sarah is not letting go. 'David, you have to understand Rabin was not a man from a good home, he was unfaithful to his wife Leah, though of course the press don't tell you that . . .' To be honest, by now, I'm tiring a bit – ignorance and dismay make an unhappy cocktail – and at lunch I try to avoid trigger words like Rabin or Bible. But at the end of the meal, we bench. One of their daughters explicates a portion of Biblical text. She tells the basic story – something about a patriarch having to go somewhere to get a wife – and then she introduces a character who is a girl aged either three or fourteen. No two rabbis, she says, have ever agreed on her age.

At once an argument starts up. Sarah says the girl can't possibly have been three because later in the story she waters ten camels. 'Have you ever tried to water a camel? The buckets are really heavy and each camel needs at least four buckets. How can a three-year-old do that?' Another daughter is rolling her eyes to the ceiling – she's the irreligious one – and one of the sons is shouting that the girl is meant to have had children: 'Are you telling me she had kids at the age of three?'

Suddenly the whole table is yelling and I am just sitting there wondering – wondering in the sense of marvelling – that it never occurs to anyone here that maybe the story is simply wrong, maybe the story-teller just got it *wrong*, but no, it's the Bible, so it must be true and it must be our fault if we don't get it and so we sit here – can we please stop *shouting* for a moment? – arguing about whether a girl of three can, or cannot, carry forty buckets to water her camels.

Who speaks for the settlers better than the brilliant Benni Begin? A few days later, he is waiting for me, on time, on schedule, at the Knesset in Jerusalem in the nice democratic canteen where people like me and Sigal and Keith can mingle with elected members of Parliament like him. When I start by asking him a question about Netanyahu, he is steely. 'This is not what you're here to talk about. You are to talk about the British Mandate.' He gets out a personal organizer, and jabs angrily at the key-pads. 'Look,' he says, 'David Hare: 2.15. Mandate.'

I swallow hard and say that the British period of rule does indeed attract me, at one stage I had wanted to research it, but that – how do I put this? – I'm a writer. I can't always predict my own interests. And my interests have deepened. Begin is still scowling. He is a slight man, with a manner which somehow seems modest and confrontational at the same time. His eyes are black as caviare. 'It's a family quarrel and I don't talk about family in front of strangers.' I say it would help me if he could explain why these conquered places mean so much to him. Why does the Oslo Accord cause him such deep offence?

Begin looks at me. He says he will answer by explaining that he has been trying to solve the problem of a notoriously difficult Ancient Hebrew message on a stone from the time of the destruction of the First Temple in 587 BC. What has interested him is how instantly familiar the stone seemed. 'It was in the language of the Book of Kings and of Samuel. The prose was a little higher than the prose I use every day, yet I felt very comfortable with it. When it said harvest, I could see the harvest. I knew the weather. I knew the smells and the seasons. I had read books about this stone, but no stranger had ever brought it close to me. The closeness I felt was a revelation.

'So you see, David, what you call the emotion of these places is, to me, the very history of our people. In these places, we feel this is Israel, this is us. Most of what matters in Jewish history happened within twenty miles of Jerusalem. We can even identify rocks where David fought against the Philistines. The exact place where Amos preached. It is inconceivable to be deprived of our right to live there and walk there; to be where our kings ruled and where our judges judged; and most important, to walk the hillsides where our prophets prophesied. This is ours because this is us. We're crippled without it.'

I say yes, I understand this – this yearning, this two-thousand-year spiritual yearning to go home – but that my time in the settlements has disturbed me. I have met people who are choosing danger, who choose to live in a place of danger, and yet who refuse to negotiate themselves out of that danger. Isn't this a form of madness, to live with no conception of the future? 'If you mean, will we give up land, then no. I have always warned "Give up the land and you will not get peace. You will get insecurity." People used to say, well, it's a gamble worth taking. And now they see the results. Two hundred and sixty people killed since Oslo, thousands injured and all because we made an accommodation with an alliance of terrorists and hoodlums. The more land you give away, the more terrorism there is. Every hectare conceded to the PLO or Islamic Jihad becomes a haven of immunity. What we have to confront is the ominous possibility of encouraging a terrorist state right next door to us.

'When you see the Nobel Peace Prize pinned on the chest of a man whose maps still don't depict the state of Israel, then you know there is nothing you can do. The hyena never changes his spots.' I say, this is crazy. Where is the hope? What is the way forward? 'The only hope now' – he sips his coffee – 'is the passage of time. Arafat can never be the solution, because he will always be the problem. As long as my Arab neighbours go on choosing him, there is no hope whatsoever.

'People know this. They know it but they don't want to face it. They go round saying "Oh wouldn't it be nice if it all worked out somehow?" They know the facts but they refuse to draw the conclusion. It won't work out.'

We are all taken aback by Begin, his intellectual command, his profound and daunting pessimism, and Sigal has gone into one of her silent moods, as if the effort of listening without interrupting has terminally lowered her spirits. Keith, meanwhile, is irrepressibly himself. Israeli rhetoric always reminds him of the lottery. It's all about numbers. He says, watch for the frequency with which '48, '67, '73 and '93 keep coming up.

Of course the reason for Keith's cheerfulness may well be that today is the day he gets rid of me. As soon as I pass out of Israel, I must be given new British Council minders. For today we are heading south via Erez, the crossing-place into Gaza.

Nothing prepares you for the physical shock of the passage. One writer has said that driving from Israel into the Gaza strip is like moving from California into

Bangladesh. You become so used to the broad highways and the easy sensuality of Israel that it is the sight of dust, sudden dust, an unholy big brown storm of pure dirt, nothing else, which alerts you to the fact that you are about to enter a society where people earn precisely eight per cent of what their opposite numbers earn in Israel.

Keith and I set off on foot across the concrete strip which divides the two countries. For a moment, it is like a John Le Carré movie, as we carry our bags past gun towers down the wide, empty road. And at the exact half-way point, just as in the movies, I am seized, bundled into a waiting car and driven quickly away, admittedly by two friendly young Englishwomen.

The reason for this haste, it turns out, is that Susannah and Pauline, my new handlers, have just told me that in twenty minutes I will be meeting with Haider Abdel Shafi. Shafi is the most popular politician in Gaza and it is something of a mystery why he has agreed to see me, since he sees no one. This news fills me with a panic which is purely and simply colonial. For months my mind has been on Israel, only Israel. Now I am being rushed towards the unique privilege of an audience with one of Palestine's most revered politicians, *and I know fuck all*.

However, as we travel along a potholed track – you couldn't call it a road – towards the city of Gaza, I am taken aback by what I am seeing. Gaza is an area forty-five kilometres by eight. Even now, one third of it is held by the Israelis, on behalf of just six thousand religious settlers. Around them are crammed three-quarters of a million Palestinians, half of whom live in the refugee camps, which were temporarily established in 1948.

Looking out at the piles of rotting garbage, the half-finished houses, the filth and the desolation, Susannah tells me that whatever shock I am feeling has been shared

25

by Yasser Arafat and his entourage. After the Oslo Accord they came out of a lifetime's exile in cities of alcohol and entertainment like Tunis and found themselves in one of the world's most conservative cultures. Although there are now a few hotels and a couple of restaurants, the few women you see are covered from head to toe. You see almost no one after seven. In Gaza, the atmosphere of the *intifada* prevails.

Dusk comes down and we have stepped back sixty years. As we push past the donkeys Pauline says, 'It's a good day because it's not been raining. When it rains, there's no drainage and the main street can be three feet in water. Turds float past the car window,' she says. There are rudiments of civilization – yellow dustbins, donated by the European Union; eighteen sets of traffic lights, donated by the French; and in a bizarre job creation scheme there are innumerable young boys dressed as policemen, and universally ignored. 'I sort of prefer that,' says Pauline. 'Inactive police are better than the bloody offensive Israeli police.'

As soon as we are ushered into Haider Abdel Shafi's elegant living-room, it becomes clear why he has agreed to meet me. He believes that I am the *Guardian* journalist, David Hirst, and, as such, the author of a recent two-page exposé straplined *Shameless in Gaza*. Since Shafi has lately resigned from the legislative body in protest at the notorious corruption of Arafat's regime, he is keen to congratulate me on my work. It seems somehow appropriate to this peculiar, hushed city that a person who knows nothing is now about to interview someone who thinks he is someone else.

It is not hard to see why Shafi is so popular. In his seventies and superbly handsome, he comes across as the apogee of the white-haired patrician Arab, serving us

Turkish coffee, and wearing a silver Savile Row suit. What's more, he is unfazed by the confusion, and happy to answer any question I may have. When he speaks against Arafat, it is with the confidence of a man who knows he is too powerful to touch.

'If I want to find excuses for Arafat, I suppose I can say he has spent his whole life in a liberation movement, and he is unused to not getting his way. Hundreds of millions of dollars have simply disappeared. Arafat is a man who buys people's allegiance. But in a society where law is neglected and never enforced, nothing can ever be right.

'Everyone understood that Arafat and his friends had had a hard life. But when they came to Gaza they were given far beyond what is reasonable. Villas, cars, phone lines. Do you wonder they are resented by those who have been here all along?'

I ask what effect the lawlessness is having on the peace process. He laughs. 'There is no peace process. By even pretending that there is such a thing, we play into Israeli hands. I was in Washington for twenty months negotiating, so I know how Israelis think. Their position has never changed. All they are doing is using physical facts to establish their presence in the land, and then to treat it as a *fait accompli*. It's a strategy, nothing more.' How does Arafat feel? 'I have no idea. He refuses to reveal his thinking. Friends say he is depressed. I cannot wonder he is depressed.'

Shafi gets up to offer chocolates from a big tin of Milk Tray. He twinkles at the ladies, who glow back from the sofa. 'President Clinton has no interest in the indigenous people of Palestine, who were here long before the Israelis arrived. He wants settlement-building to stop. But for him it's not a matter of principle. It's a tactic in his peace process. It's a pause he wants, not a stop.

'Our most urgent task is to reform ourselves. It's far more important than negotiation with Israel. You can't get anywhere if you live in a society without principles. When Mohammed came back from battle, he said, "We come back from the little strife and we return to the bigger strife." They asked him what he meant. "The strife of the soul." But of course nowadays, nobody thinks of these things.'

It is Shafi's achievement to create a calm in us all, and the calm lasts as we step out on to the empty street. I ask, 'Where does Arafat live?' It's dark and not a soul moves. We drive towards the sea. We turn. A quiet avenue of villas. At the end of this road of seaside vernacular are two enormous tanks. Arafat's house, looking like any other.

We get out. Silence. Only the roar of the surf, the Mediterranean. 'There'll be a civil war,' says Pauline. 'It's inevitable. The society is simply not functioning.'

Keith had warned me to expect the British Council officers to have gone native. A previous one wouldn't even speak to his counterpart in Tel Aviv. Solidarity, you see. But these two women are not dewy-eyed. Back at our boarding-house, the owner and her son are sitting around in the lobby reviling an art-event which has happened earlier. A huge painted billboard has been unveiled at the Erez crossing, supposedly as a plea for peace, but actually the work of a bullshit Australian artist whose use of gratuitous Christian symbolism – flocks of white doves and so on – has managed to offend almost everyone. But when they attack it, delightedly detailing every element in the fiasco, Susannah lays into them, saying this is typically Palestinian, always wanting things to fail and being pleased when they do.

Later, as I try innocently to get the boarding-house owner's parrot to speak English, it is Susannah's friend

Pauline who finally sets me straight. Pauline is here to help the Palestinians set up a civil service. 'What you're seeing, I'm afraid, is the result of the *intifada*. You have to understand that was a real revolution, and it came up from below, not from the leadership. But now . . . well, it's like that film with Meryl Streep. What's it called?' 'You mean the one where she's meant to be Danish?' 'No, not that one. The one set during the war.' 'Oh, *Plenty*,' I say. 'I wrote it.' She looks at me suspiciously. 'Well, anyway, the figure of the woman – what's she called?' 'Susan Traherne.' 'Yes, the woman who goes to war at twenty and for whom the peace is this terrible disappointment. It's the same here. It's like *Plenty*. These kids were thirteen or fourteen, some of them even seven or eight, and they found they could create their own structures. They could have a direct and devastating effect on daily life in Israel. By their actions they truly achieved something. But now the energy is gone. The men from Tunis came and stole it. Those same kids have grown up and are sitting around in cafés. They have no life, they have no jobs, and they're totally disillusioned.

'There was a point once, there was a reason. You were fighting for a Palestinian state, and you were willing to die. What on earth would you die for now? If you struggled now, you would be arrested, and tortured and put to death, all so that Arafat can go on being corrupt. There are more people in prison today under Arafat than there were under the Israelis! What's the point of dying for a society without rules? If the Israelis were really clever, they would give the Palestinians every inch of land they want, and then stand by and watch them fuck it up.'

This is a terrible analysis, but it's confirmed when I next travel, this time to the Arab city of Ramallah. My official companion is Muna Khlefi, a sparkling, clever Palestinian who thinks I am incredibly lucky to have met Haider

Abdel Shafi and who wants to hear every word. Her eyes light up. 'He is a great man. He is the guts, he is the soul of the country. The new leadership just want to do business. They did business in Lebanon, they did it in Tunis. They say: just make money, then later we'll decide what kind of society we want. But Shafi says you cannot delay this question.'

Muna asks me now why I've come to the Middle East. I say, it's hard to explain. It's an instinct. Playwrights are drawn to places without quite knowing why. Most of my work has come from just poking about. Muna looks at me. 'That's not a good enough answer. Do you really know what you're doing here?' I say, yes, perhaps I'm beginning to.

Muna wants me to meet Albert Aghazerin, the great Palestinian historian, and talk to him about the problem of Jerusalem. He is late, so I sit in his outer office at Birzeit University, looking out on to the hillside campus. I pick up the Amnesty International report on Palestine. 'Subjects have been electrocuted, hung upside down. Scalding plastic has been melted over their bodies . . .'

After an hour, Aghazerin arrives, a frightening figure with a big pipe and a superb sculpted face, rather like the actor Hugh Griffith. He thrusts an article at me, ordering me to read it. When I dare to ask a question, he sighs and says, 'Where do you start? For me, you can only answer this by considering the Egyptian conquest of 1831', and sets off on a canter through nineteenth-century statistics which I can't grasp, partly because he scares me so much, and partly because his mind is leaping about like an angry gazelle.

However, when I ask him what he thinks the religious Jew truly believes, he starts to cheer up, pleased that we turn out to share a common interest. 'All the apocalyptic stuff only starts after 1967. You do get a smell of it before, but it's only after the Six Day War that the Jews come up with this new interpretation of the Bible. The building of the Third Temple! The end of the world! It's pure opportunism. Religious revelation which just happens to be the most perfect political connivance.

'There are women in Jerusalem who've actually started sewing the garments for the priests of the Third Temple and they're preparing the unblemished . . . *animal*. You know, what is it? That . . . what is it? Animal, begins with "h"? *H*!,' he shouts. 'Heifer?' 'That's right! *Heifer*! They are preparing the unblemished *heifer* to purge the temple. And of course it all suits Israel fine. But groups like this always bring violence and bloodshed. Rabin's assassination did not come out of nothing.'

I ask if he thinks Israel divided. 'Deeply, deeply divided. There are three Israels now. The hedonistic Israel of Tel Aviv. The austere Israel of Jerusalem. And the mad Israel of Hebron which wants only vengeance and blood.

'Look I do not discount what the Jews suffered. Nobody can. I know what they suffered in Europe. But to me it is as if they jumped from a burning building and they happened to land and break the neck of a man who was passing. And when the man says, "Hey, you've broken my neck", they say, "Sorry, it's because of the fire." And when the man says, "Yes, but my neck's broken", they just break his arm in order to try and shut him up. And when he doesn't shut up, they break his other arm. Then they break his leg. Then his other leg. All in the hope that one day he'll shut up. But, you see, I don't think he will.

'I like these parables. I will give you another. Israel has its hand round our throat. It can't throttle us, but nor can it let us go. He's unhappy because he wants to go for a beer, and we're unhappy because we're being strangled, but in some terrible way we're both bound up in each other's unhappiness. We cannot be separated.'

I ask him if it will change. 'It will stink before it changes. You have to ask about the so-called peace process: is its purpose the exchange of land, or is it the subjugation of the Palestinian people? Because, on the ground, there's no question that the evidence points to the second. What is the reason for all these stupid checkpoints, and the impossibility of Arabs getting a visa to visit Jerusalem? Arabs can't visit Jerusalem! On the ground what do we actually see? Nothing but the security state and its apparatus of harassment.'

'The Israelis no longer have a political aim,' he says, 'just security'. On the road to Jerusalem the other night he was stopped, as he always is, at the checkpoint. The army girl who was no older than his own daughter started to go through all his luggage. When she put his things back he said, 'Do you like what you do? I have a daughter, and I will give her the right to do many things, but not this, because it's dehumanizing.' Do you know what she replied? 'I don't think about it. Now goodbye.'

'Shall I sum it up for you? They always ask two questions. Did you pack the bag yourself? Did anyone give you anything to carry? The other day when they asked the first question, I answered and I added, "And no one gave me anything to carry." The Israeli guard looked at me angrily: "How dare you? Don't you know? You are not allowed to answer the second question until I ask it."

'David, that says it all.'

Albert and I part firm friends. He implores me to look up the Palestinian ambassador on my return to London. 'First-class envoy, really first-class.' And my own spirits are reflected in the cheerful air of Ramallah, the largest

Arab city in the West Bank, where women wear dresses and where alcohol is served in the restaurants.

On the way to the Presto Café, where I am to meet the producer of *Romeo and Juliet*, Muna explains that George Ibrahim is one of the few people in Palestine allowed to make theatre. On arrival, George turns out to be bear-like and convivial, punching my arm whenever he makes a good point. As good points arrive at thirty-second intervals, I end up significantly bruised.

'When we did *Romeo and Juliet*, at the end I knew I had been used. Not by Eran personally, of course, but by the Israelis. I would never do it again. Least of all now. But let me tell you this' – he leans forward to reveal the ultimate secret – 'artistically we were better. Our side was better by the certification of everyone who saw the play.'

Before he can say more we are joined by one of George's best friends, the forty-two-year-old poet of the *intifada*, Hussein Barghouti. With his long straggly hair and his chainsmoking intensity, I instantly recognize Barghouti as a figure who has tragically disappeared from British life, but whom you still see in Paris and Berlin: the genuine, twenty-four-carat intellectual, arms waving and high as a kite on ideas.

George stokes the fire by attacking the portrayal of Arabs in Western films. 'We are always just puppets. You play with us according to your imagination, so we are monkeys smoking pipes, or more usually, criminals. I hate Hamas myself, so I know that extremists *are* criminals. But I also know why. I know *why* they commit crimes. Just think of it. Think! Think what depths of despair it will take to make you walk into a market with lumps of dynamite tied round your chest. But no American film-maker has ever tried to think. All Arabs get lumped together.'

Hussein joins in. 'Did you see *The English Patient*? Foreground action: white people, noble, fine feelings, strong, full of laughter, walking in gardens, taking showers, *standing up*! Background action: Arabs, shifty, mysterious, dirty, untrustworthy, *sitting down*! Or *Air Force One*! This picture explains to us what Arabs want. What do they want? To capture the American President! Why? Why would anyone want an American President? Why would they do it? No, really? The reason? Because the world needs an enemy. When the Soviet Union was around, there it was, ready-made. Now it's to be us. It suits the Americans to say, "Who are the Arabs? The Arabs are the people who will start the Third World War."

'You know, I have been reading Mishima and he is very moving on this subject. The destruction of Japanese culture by the West. The West injecting violence into a culture. All the conflicts in this area are imported. They are not organic. What is the state of Israel but the transformation of native Semitic culture into a terrible Western caricature? Plus, of course, the added horror of nuclear weapons. Consider: this area is where the world's great religions all originate. The West collected its religion from here. Yet how did that religion come back to us? In the form of the Crusades! You take your religion from this part of the world, then you bring it back to us as violence.'

George is looking restless, so I make sure my next question is about theatre, to give George a go. 'In theatre now, it is very hard to know what plays to do,' George says. 'You cannot just choose a play. Because every play raises the question: why do this one? What relevance does it have? And all the actors start arguing. During the *intifada* plays just seemed silly because 100, 000 people were shot.' Hussein interrupts. 'I was shot!' George replies irritably. 'We all know! We all know you were shot! No, you need writers to write about what is happening now, because there is no other subject. I tried to get Hussein to write a play, but we did not agree.' Hussein grins, proud. 'We did not agree because I don't deal with audiences.' 'No. Exactly! You don't!'

Hussein I'm not interested in the audience.

George He's right! He isn't!

Hussein I'm a poet. I make a good artistic text. I don't think about how it will be received. I just send it out, into the air.

Hussein That's why his play was no good. In the theatre, in all theatre, the audience is the purpose. Only the audience can give the play meaning. He can't accept that.

Hussein I will never accept that!

George He needs to go to class. I need to send him to class to teach him to write a play.

Hussein is beaming, and I can tell he isn't going to go. After a lifetime in the theatre I half-share his doubts. If only a play could be half-play, half-poem! The two of them now embrace. Hussein turns to me. 'This has been a typical Palestinian conflict. No search for common ground whatsoever. George thinks what he thinks and I think what I think. But George still wants me around. Why? Because if I weren't around, life would be boring.'

I'm happy in Ramallah, it's less desperate, less disturbing than Gaza, but every night I travel back to Jerusalem, where not only half the world's religions started but also – hardly by coincidence – where the world first started collecting crime statistics. Yes, Crime Number One. Cain killed Abel. It happened in Jerusalem. And ever since, the story is of massacre and of bloodshed.

35

At Oslo, the question of how Jerusalem should be administered was put to one side as being simply too difficult even to approach. For this Jerusalem is the world capital of claim and counter-claim, the acknowledged metropolis of dispute. Here, contention, abrasion and mistrust are scored deep into the subtly pink rock.

'The angry face of Yahweh', says Arthur Koestler, 'broods over hot rocks which have seen more holy murder, rape and plunder than any other place on earth.' 'The air over Jerusalem', says Herman Melville, 'is saturated with prayers and dreams . . . it's hard to breathe.' For me, there's no question: I have to walk the Via Dolorosa, to follow the Stations of the Cross, which represent the steps on Christ's journey to his death. 'All these stones, all this sadness, all this light.' It's the religion of my homeland, even if homeland's not a word I've ever used. But the shock is to realise just how little impact Christianity has made. It's amusing to see busloads of American evangelicals, dressed in shell suits and baseball caps, expecting Universal Studios and instead searching vainly in an old Arab city for any remaining evidence of Our Lord. 'There ought to be more. What's happened? Why is there not more?'

To be honest, I share their bewilderment. After all, Christianity's quite a well-known religion and I'd say influential in its time. You'd think it was still worth a pilgrimage, but in this town we come a sporting third. We're the sideshow. The Via Dolorosa is a pavement which winds unimpressively past postcard shops and up narrow alleys, filling me with a sense of loss, with a tangible sense of something lost – until it reaches the Church of the Holy Sepulchre which – wouldn't you know, wouldn't you just guess it? – is also disputed. Yes, even the church which contains the stone where Our Lord was crucified is shared unhappily: seventy per cent to the Greeks and the rest doled out higgledy-piggledy between the Armenian Christians, the Coptic Christians, the Latins, the Syrians and the Ethiopians. A people divided by a common religion. Sects and the single Church.

And what's more – hold on, here we go – is the stone, in fact, on the right spot? Nobody knows. Archaeologists also dispute. Nobody *can* know because nobody knows where the city walls were. Nobody agrees. Where was Calvary indeed? So for now – look, is anything certain? – let's just do as the family next to me and drop alarmingly to our knees, on the working assumption – let's just *assume* – X marks the spot, and kiss the stone. After all, does the literal truth of it matter? Does the literal truth matter? Aren't we kissing an idea? Stones or ideas? Stones or ideas?

And it's a relief, I'd say a relief, to come out of the dark and stroll down to the big open plaza where you find the Wailing Wall, strangely impressive, tall, uncrowded, the bit where the Jews are allowed. For towering above them, at the very top of the arrangement, is the most coveted spot in the universe of faith, what the Jews call Temple Mount, but what to the Arabs who occupy it is known as the Haram al-Sharif. And at its centre, the saffron-yellow golden Dome of the Rock.

I have felt since I arrived that Jerusalem doesn't need my admiration. Enough people are obsessed with it already. The truth is, I look at it and think how beautiful it must have been when it was a small town. Myself, I would like Jerusalem more if it weren't so important. But even I, inside the Arab sanctuary, taking in the cleanest, most oxygenated sun-dazzled air you ever breathed, looking across to the Mount of Olives, yield to the splendour of the place and realize: oh I see, how provoking it is to own beauty, to own the most breathtaking space of them all.

Coming down, Sigal is waiting. I haven't seen the delightful Sigal for some time, because I have been, as it were, with the other lot, and so she is spilling over with gossip: Netanyahu's government is falling, or is about to fall, or may not fall, because some Russian assistant is or isn't implicated in some scandal about money and loans. I get into the car. The driver doesn't know the city, so we circle for some time. It's interesting. When we stop people in the street to ask them the way to Yad Vashem, the world-famous museum of the Holocaust, some of them don't seem to know.

The museum's power is in its very simplicity, a bleak photographic record ending not, as Westerners expect, in 1945, but in 1948 with the foundation of the state. At the centre of the display, I stop at the text of Himmler's speech, the most astonishing document of the war, in which he congratulates his men on the discipline they have shown in exerting what he calls their 'moral right' to exterminate the Jews.

It is, Himmler says, 'natural tact' which prevents any German from speaking of what they are doing. Himmler knows it is hard work, digging pits and throwing bodies into them. But what he is proudest of is that in doing this work his men have – the phrase resonates down the century – his men have 'stayed decent', and it is staying decent 'that has made us hard'.

The only false notes in the museum are hit by works of art. Sculpture and painting. They seem superfluous. In every case the gesture seems inadequate. What is a painting, a painting of a starving man? What is a painting of a corpse? It's the facts we want. Give us the facts.

We go into the darkness, into the Hall of Names. Here, every Jew who is known to have died between 1939 and 1945 is given a simple file. Finally, after so many years, numbers are given the dignity of becoming human beings. In this sombre room of open shelves, the scale of the Nazi offence, its deliberateness is revealed. The unbroken rank of documentation hits you more shockingly, more woundingly, than any other image.

We walk in the Garden of Remembrance. We begin to feel the sun. Voltaire said you have to choose between countries where you sweat and countries where you think. The confusing thing about Israel is that it's one where you do both. And my mind is racing now. We're all blind. We all see only what we want to. Don't we blank out the rest?

And me more than anyone. At times I'm the worst of the lot. I've seen a good many politicians while I'm here but at the end I'm due to meet one who's lost all hope of office. I'm used to hours getting past the security arrangements for the Minister of Something or Other, but my last visit is to a tiny, unsecured basement in Tel Aviv. I have already noticed that just the name of Shulamit Aloni is enough to attract violent hostility from some who knew her as the flaming red firebrand of the Rabin government. And when she comes, already talking, into the room she is like a manic-depressive Melina Mercouri with thick glasses and no time to wait for the questions.

'What you want to know?' she asks, throwing herself down into the biggest chair. 'Why do you say it's difficult to understand what's happening? It couldn't be simpler. We're going backwards. What's so difficult to understand? The Jews were once victims, so now we are brainwashed to believe we will always be victims and victims can do no wrong. Suddenly we've become strong and greedy and pretend we can justify everything. We're told all the time the Palestinians want to throw us into the sea. We have six million people and the strongest army in the region.

And yet we speak of them as if they were two equal powers. It's just manipulating people's fears.'

She raps out an order in Hebrew for Sigal to go and get some coffee. Sigal gets up, furious, while Shulamit carries on, blaming the reversal entirely on Netanyahu. I am enjoying Shulamit – she is absolutely, as they say, my cup of tea – but even I am a little surprised by her blaming Netanyahu for everything. Are things ever really down to one man? 'You are English and I assume you went to high school,' she says, rather nastily, 'so you will have heard of the philosopher Hobbes. Hobbes says a whole society can be destroyed by a single individual who decides to come along and burn down the forest. Netanyahu, aided by the greedy Fascists, the army, the security service, is such a man.'

I ask what she can do meanwhile. Does she just wait? 'To wait means to die. I have no optimistic things to tell you. Why come to me? What are you doing here? Go to the younger people and ask them what they think.' She is staring at me, as if it's the first time she's noticed me at all. 'Why you write down my blah-blah?'

I say that I normally start an interview by explaining what I am doing here, but somehow we had jumped that stage. 'It's a bad time. What can I say?' 'It's what you feel.' 'No, it's not what I feel. It's what I know. If it were only what I feel I'd go and have a brandy and I'd feel better. I'm not telling you my mood, though my mood is bad. I'm telling you the facts. I am gloomy. But what do I matter?'

She looks me in the eye, challenging me to defy her. This talented lawyer, who has done as much as anyone to offer practical support to the victims of discrimination and seg-regation, is now lost, in pain, painfully lost and spoiling for a fight. 'What do you see happening next?' 'Demonstrations, bloodshed, bitterness. It's not yet a civil war, but it's a form of civil war. It's a *Kulturkampf*. Do you know what that is?' I nod. 'We are in the middle of one. The great mistake was to give power to the clergy in the first place. And immigrants came from Eastern Europe and the Mediterranean, they were backward, they knew nothing about democracy. They think democracy is the rule of the majority. What's worst, we have no written constitution . . .' I have not opened my mouth and already she is shouting at me. 'Don't tell me you don't have one in England! I know that! I know that! But you have the Magna Carta and Oliver Cromwell and a tradition, and until recently you had the idea that certain things are not done.'

She gets up. It ends as abruptly as it begins. 'Anything else? I have to run.' I am aware this woman's world was destroyed by Rabin's assassination. She shakes my hand. 'The British caused a lot of problems here.' 'I know that,' I say. 'Do you know what I say to the British? Since you left, we love you very much. And I mean it. We do.'

We walk back to the British Council, Sigal fuming at the way Shulamit insulted her, and apologizing for her manner. I say it didn't bother me at all. I'm just a pen.

I start collating my notes in the office. A British Council worker comes in, called George. He is a Christian Arab. 'He is my enemy, ' says Sigal and they both roar with laughter contentedly. Shulamit Aloni rings to ask us both to pardon her for being what she calls 'impatient and obnoxious'. She is worn down, she says, by the weight of her case-work.

We set off for the airport. On the way in, I have been advised not to let them stamp my passport so that I can visit Arab countries. But, on the way out, before I can say a word, *wham*, not a second to speak, and the word *Israel* is on my passport for ever.

41

At this point the lights shift, and the feel of the stage is changed for the epilogue.

Gatwick. My plane is late. I return in the middle of the night. I get on the train to Victoria. Darkness. Via Dolorosa.

The power of Simenon, someone observes, is that he always travelled through France by barge. From the canals, he saw only the backs of houses, the backs of streets, the backs of churches.

The Israeli military commander, unnamed at his own request, who sits across a desk smiling, telling me that only 20,000 Jews have been killed in the cause of setting up the state. 'Not that every death isn't a tragedy, please don't misunderstand me, and of course I'm not talking about the Jewish experience in Europe. But the Jewish experience in this part of the world? 20,000 to set up a whole country: that's not so bad, you know. Not bad. Not for a whole state.'

Victoria deserted. Into a black cab. Up past Buckingham Palace, Park Lane, and north up the Finchley Road. Passion receding up the broad tree-lined streets. Fitzjohns Avenue. Via Dolorosa.

Haider Abdel Shafi quoting Mohammed on his return from battle. 'I come back from the little strife and I return to the greater. The strife of the soul.'

Netanyahu on the radio saying that like all the century's greatest men he is aware of being misunderstood. Then naming Kirk Douglas as a brick in the Wailing Wall.

Sitting in the harbour with Eran Baniel, eating fish. 'Fuck the land! Fuck it! What does the land matter? The highest value to a Jew is human life. The idea that stones now

42

matter more than lives is a complete deformation of the Jewish religion. A deformation!'

Left on Chapel Street. Tall terraces of impeccable Georgian houses on either side. I think of David Grossman walking on the Heath. 'I have some sort of mineral reaction,' he said.

Pauline, in the boarding-house in Gaza: 'There was a point once, there was a reason. You were fighting for a Palestinian state, and you were willing to die. What on earth would you die for now?'

The taxi turns right and right again. Are we where we live, or are we what we think? What matters? Stones or ideas? Stones or ideas?

My dog Blanche waking in the night to greet me, the heavy white door of my home closing behind me.

Via Dolorosa.

When Shall We Live?

'When Shall We Live?', the eleventh Eric Symes Abbot Memorial Lecture, was delivered by David Hare at Westminster Abbey on 9 May 1996 and subsequently at Keble College, Oxford.

Although, for me, it is plainly a great privilege to be asked to give this year's Eric Symes Abbot Memorial lecture, I can well understand if there are those among you who are contemplating the choice of the present speaker with a certain bewilderment. I must admit that as I prepared to speak, I have shared a good deal of that bewilderment myself. The Church of England is distinguished by its exceptionally non-doctrinaire and generous attitude to those who do not share its own most sacred beliefs. For better or worse, it is nothing if it is not a liberal church. But even so, I can see that it is quite striking that the Dean of Westminster should invite an obvious heathen to speak in memory of a man who, from what I have read of him, seems chiefly marked out from other men by the power of his Christian faith and example.

The oddness of the invitation does not stop there. Westminster Abbey is what is called a Royal Peculiar. That means that it is not under the jurisdiction of any Bishop. Least of all, I was told, in a tone which betrayed an almost Trollopian intensity of feeling, is it, God forbid, under the authority of the Bishop of London. The Queen herself is technically known as the Abbey's Visitor. But it is as a wholehearted, even slightly obsessive republican that I stand here, making my remarks in a church which, even for me, is most movingly full of the evidence of its own intimate connections with monarchs, living and dead.

Those of us who believe and have long argued that the hacking death-rattle of royalty is obscuring other, more positive noises in Great Britain are well used to the abuse we attract from our impassioned opponents. Yet even I was intrigued by the line of attack taken against us in a recent edition of the *Guardian*. The article had started with the routine attempts to type enemies of the Palace as embittered no-hopers, themselves intent on taking over the running of the country and crazed by the heady prospect of drinking their kir and eating their olives with their literary cronies on the balcony of Buckingham Palace. But as the journalist went on, he reported a rather more interesting argument and one which served to bring me up short. The entertaining royalist historian Andrew Roberts, whose book about the followers of Churchill I admired as much as anyone, was reported as saying that there was one crucial difference between monarchists and republicans, a difference which indicated to any honest observer which side must finally be in the right: that whereas monarchists were, as a group, willing to die for their beliefs, republicans plainly weren't.

In saying this, of course, Roberts was trying to establish that constitutional reform of any kind is a concern of what the press in its most self-hating and exhausted cliché likes to call 'the chattering classes'. Faith in the Queen, Roberts implied, was in some way a true emotion, whereas faith in democracy must, by contrast, be a phoney one. But it seemed to me an odd way for an historian to vindicate his own case, and indeed one which might unintentionally put him in some distinctly dubious company. Active service members of the IRA, wreaking their random bombings on the city streets, are, after all, willing to die for their beliefs. The lunatics of Hamas, who murder women and children in Jerusalem, are willing to die for their beliefs. Japanese kamikazes, firing killer-sprays on the Tokyo underground, are willing to die for their beliefs. I began at once to form the picture of a portly young historian with barrels of dynamite tied round his chest, going to blow himself up at a meeting of Charter 88, and all in the interests of defending the uneasy House of Windsor.

Beneath this happy image lies what I hope is an important idea, and one which I intend to provide the starting-point of this lecture: that most of us, indeed, do have little idea of what we believe, and are also extremely confused on the subject of whether we would be willing to die for it. Somewhere, in nearly every theological volume I have read, it is asserted that the most important decision any person has to make on earth is what form of supreme being he or she does or does not believe in. Yet the mystery of this supposed urgent subject is just how many days, weeks, or indeed years so many of us pass quite contentedly without once being troubled by it. Although you might feel the question of God's nature and existence *ought* to be obsessively important to each and every one of us, the simple fact of the modern world is that it is not felt to be. At least until the approach of death, the majority of Westerners are willing to tick the box in which they profess that they have some generalized religious belief but they are jiggered if they can actually say what it is.

This is, at first glance, a peculiar state of affairs. It is also one for which I do not think the conventional explanations quite hold water. The usual means of arguing away the modern indifference to conventional religion is to assert that because we in the West now live thirty years longer than we did even a hundred years ago, and because we endure less physical suffering, we have therefore lost some crucial sense of what life is actually about. In the Middle Ages, it is said, death was all around. People had an inborn sense of how transitory their existence was. They knew they were not here for long. For that reason their minds were wonderfully focused on the question of where they might be going next. They also knew the unspeakable horror of unrelieved pain and the sharp cruelty of sudden death. So they had no problem, it is said, in directing their minds towards a place where human loss might be explained and, hopefully, relieved. But now, it is argued, comfort and even luxury have inured us to considering the shortness and harshness of our span on earth. The soothing apparatus of our hospitals, the bright lights in our shopping malls, the constant chatter of our television sets and the general anaesthetic prosperity of our surroundings all combine to protect us from brute physical unpleasantness, which was once such a powerful spur to religious fear, if not to religious understanding.

I must say I have some difficulty with this argument. Like many people, I find it hard to admire a God who feels the need to make life short and brutal in order for His creation to appreciate Him better. I have my doubts about a religious faith which depends on human deprivation and hardship for it to achieve a suitable intensity. If the only way we can be moved to believe in God is by experiencing the very worst aspects of the world He has created, then I have very grave difficulties with what kind of God He must therefore be. If human beings are, as Christianity claims, put on this earth to worship God and to do His will, it seems an extraordinary state of affairs that they should need to be reminded of that purpose only by the bitterness and brevity of their own lives.

The other way, of course, that the Church consoles itself for the apparent lack of interest in its own affairs is by asserting that there is an overall loss of belief in the idea of authority itself. While I was researching my play about the Church of England, *Racing Demon*, which started life at the National Theatre over six years ago, then I was told by a number of inner-city vicars that we lived in what they were happy to call a post-Christian era. The Church was a victim of the general scepticism which characterized the age. It was, you could say, just one more British institution which no longer commanded automatic respect. I was also constantly reassured by the vicars themselves that they were perfectly happy with this state of affairs. Indeed, some of them even welcomed it. Jesus,

one South London rector told me, was a friend of the
weak, so that if the Church of England itself was in a
weakened condition, one might even say this was a good
thing rather than a bad one. It helped the Church to a
true Christian compassion. Nothing, he assured me, could
be more dangerous than a Church triumphant, as in the
Victorian age, for that way lay arrogance and compla-
cency. Shuddering with horror when describing the
excesses of the American churches of the South, he con-
gratulated himself on the fact that the Church of England
with its declining attendances, rotting buildings and half-
hearted theology, was mercifully in no danger of being led
astray by any vulgar or excessive popularity.

Besides, I was frequently told, even if people did not
actually go to church, it was obvious however that they
did have some residual spiritual sense. Even those in one
parish who never attended the actual services had been
distressed when they saw the old church pews out on the
pavement waiting to be replaced. They feared something
was being lost, even if they themselves never actually went
as far as using it. Why should a priest worry if spirituality
expressed itself locally by less formal means than weekly
attendance at the ever-changing, subtly depressing rituals
of the Church of England? At times of disaster people
gravitated gratefully towards religious buildings. They
still felt instinctively that there was something numinous,
something holy about a place where, even if you cannot
believe yourself, many people have at least believed before
you. Although individuals were no longer willing to subscribe to a code – because we lived in an era where codes
were all so hopelessly discredited – they did however con-
tinue to wrestle with spiritual problems which brought
them, most especially at times of birth, marriage and
death, towards a house where they knew these crucial
things would be honoured. People, in short, were still religious in spite of themselves.

Once again, I am not sure if I want to buy shares in this popular line of argument. Plainly, only an imbecile would deny that we in the West no longer invest much faith in authority. The reason is dazzlingly simple. In my lifetime, authority has not done much to deserve it. As the author of a matching play about the law, *Murmuring Judges*, I am hardly in a position to deny that a mixture of anger and cynicism now characterizes people's attitude, for example, to the criminal justice system. The shocking travesties of justice – most of them racially motivated – which characterized the worst courtroom trials of the nineteen seventies and eighties have not led, in the nineties, to a fitting humility among politicians and the legal profession. Instead we have seen an ever-cruder vindictiveness at the Home Office. Under its current office-holder it has no aim to reform the criminal. It seeks only to slake the bloodlust of *Daily Mail* editorial-writers by doing nothing but punishing him.

As the author of a third play, this time about the Labour Party, *The Absence of War*, I also know that, at least since the election of the present leaderships, nobody has the slightest expectation that a genuine idealism will guide the programmes of the two political parties which have some chance of power. Even the ambition of inspiration is, quite simply, out of fashion. Churchill, significantly a leader at a time of war, was the last Prime Minister about whom the generality of the population entertained overwhelmingly positive feelings. Kennedy, for all his faults, remains the last President. I can also see that when leaders of whatever persuasion attempt to offer even the most hesitant guidelines to suggest a moral basis for citizens' behaviour they make themselves figures of open hilarity and contempt. At a time when you have been part of a Government which chose mendaciously to re-arm Saddam Hussein, when you have been encouraging the leaders of the privatized utilities to risk suffocation by permanent nasal immersions in the public trough, and you are constantly coming upon your own Cabinet Ministers with their trousers wrapped round their ankles, you may well be making a grave tactical error in suggesting that the time has come for the electorate to get Back to Basics.

Yet however dishonest and openly ludicrous the public climate of the time has become, and however deep people's disillusion with their leaders may be, I think this obvious ethos of distrust provides a singularly poor excuse for the frailty of the Church. Why should an institution whose concerns are meant, in part at least, to be not of this earth, feel itself so implicated in the failure of institutions which are? On the contrary, you might expect that at a time when powers temporal are so plainly failing to win the love of the populations of the West, people might very well instead have been drawn towards what was being offered by powers spiritual. If, as it seems, materialism has so sapped Western man that he has reached some sort of dispirited state at which he no longer believes that the best of his dreams and wishes can be embodied in his social ideals, then why on earth is he not turning his attention to a religion, which, in theory at least, is supposed to offer some sort of alternative to a life lived purely for money and self-advancement?

But if I cannot accept the professionals' favourite arguments for the decay of organized religion, I am however persuaded by their final line of defence, by what we may call the Church of England's ultimate fall-back position: in other words, that however incoherent our religious beliefs and practices, we are all still aware of the spiritual side of our nature. Plainly, it is true. Asked recently, like Princess Diana, though happily in less publicized circumstances, to attend some open-heart operations, I looked into the deep crimson cavity of the chest, with the red pulsating football at its centre in a lake of blood. The colours were straight out of the apocalyptic paintings of Fuseli. As

I wondered at how we carry around inside us an unseen landscape which so exactly parallels the external world, but daubed in the tones of our dreams, I experienced that familiar giddy sensation of absolute mystery. Who among us actually imagines that the human mind will ever be able to comprehend or 'explain' the universe? When scientists like Stephen Hawking confess such an ambition then clearly they make themselves absurd. The absence in us of any chance finally to comprehend our own existence makes us at every state of our lives prey to intuitions which often appear to us more real than our ordered thoughts. Yet, like many people, I am not sure if the Church of England's present arrangements always play to that sense we all have of the transcendent.

Last year, answering just such an unexplained urge in myself, I ended up alone, driving a hundred miles on a beautiful spring afternoon to visit what is almost my favourite building in England. I do not know if it is true that Oliver Cromwell really did stable his horses in Ely Cathedral, but the idea of it has always summoned up for me an image of almost unbearable power – the rebel army of the republican movement lying down in straw on that massive stone floor, men and animals all night together, with the magnificent twelfth-century pillars soaring above them into the sinister, almost primitive darkness of the vaulted ceiling. As I sped across the pancake-flat fields, I could hardly wait for the sight of that extraordinary, cold, mystic façade. On arrival I cheerfully paid the rather surprising entrance fee, only to go in and find a lot of men in shorts wandering about with walkie-talkies in one hand and drills in the other. There was no chance of peace. Whatever humiliation Cromwell had deliberately inflicted on Ely, it was as nothing compared to the Cathedral's own bizarre decision to allow the *Antiques Roadshow* to be televised there. What are the religious priorities at work when you charge visitors £2.50 to be admitted to

54

one of the most suggestive and hallucinatory church buildings in Europe, only to have the spirit of the place
destroyed by BBC carpenters banging away with hammers
and by eager townsfolk queuing up to ask whether their
granny's chamberpot will turn out to be Delft? It is
beyond farce. Yes, the Church's area of expertise is said to
be with the spiritual. But at such moments spirituality
seems to be the last thing on anyone's mind.

The Christ who threw the moneylenders out of the temple would, I think, have been as bewildered as me by an
established Church which has timidly allowed itself to
become so close to the secular institutions of the day – the
Army, the monarchy, the Government. At first sight, it
looks like an organization which now lacks the missionary
courage to set itself apart. It sounds too polite, too fright-
ened to remind us that its determining values are in fact
radically different from those of the rest of society. Yet,
even as I say this, I am also aware that the very best work
of what currently makes up the Church of England is conducted by men and women who barely make mention of
those crucial values at all.

Having been brought up in an Anglo-Catholic school
which laid great emphasis on daily, somewhat futile
reminders to the boys of their own innate sinfulness, I was
astonished when researching my play about inner London
priesthood thirty years later to meet a supremely dedicated group of men who barely mentioned, let alone
spread the Gospel in the regular pursuit of their mission.
To point out the most obvious development, they no
longer saw conversion as part of their job. Hour after
hour, day after day, there they were, out on the street,
doing the most menial and demanding kind of work. As
they helped young couples to fill in DSS forms, or advised
young blacks in trouble with the police, as they visited
old people's homes or went to arbitrate in disputes on
council estates, they served honourably as society's

troubleshooters, doing what was to all intents and purposes social work, and all on half of even a social worker's pay. But at no time did it seem part of their agenda to mention to the people they were helping that every Sunday, in another costume perhaps, they conducted services which related, however loosely, to a much-discussed incident in the Middle East two thousand years ago.

Their principle fear, they said, was of what they, in an alarming phrase, called 'stuffing Christ down people's throats'. This, they said, was something which could only 'put people off'. As soon as ordinary people heard what the priests called 'the language of Zion' – all that familiar talk about God and salvation – they were alienated. At bottom, the vicars said, that stuff was unhelpful. It was – another favourite phrase – 'linguistic baggage'. The essential message of Christianity was love. If the priests themselves could express God's love for the world through the work they undertook, it would be sheer arrogance meanwhile to dare to insist to what was now a multi-ethnic community that each member adhere to the priest's own private, culturally determined system of belief.

No one was more typical of this – one might say – defeatist tendency in the modern Church than one compelling South London vicar whose faith was dryer than the driest Martini I have ever tasted. I would say it was ninety-nine parts good work diluted by just one quick twist of doctrine. I asked him for evidence of the power of prayer, in which he said he did unexpectedly believe. Thinking for a while, he cited the example of a very sick child in his parish for whom he had kept an overnight vigil. After twelve hours of sincere pleading with God, the child, whose life had previously been hanging by a thread, had indeed been saved. Impressed by this, I asked him what he would have felt had the child died. 'Oh,' he replied contentedly, 'I'm so surprised when anything happens at all, I don't even notice the occasions when it doesn't.'

Of course this low self-esteem in the modern Church militant made, from my point of view, for wonderful drama. To be frank, I had fun. The play was timely. At that moment the well of public values in Britain was being poisoned by an influential government, itself stacked with millionaires, and therefore self-righteously intent on preaching the virtues of acquisition to others. So it was touching to meet a distinctive body of clerics who were so plainly motivated by concerns other than career or money. But I must admit it was also delightful comedy to come upon a Christian institution which seemed terrified of mentioning its own founder's name. A Labour Party which does not dare use the word 'socialism' is one thing. But a church which does not dare say 'Christ' is quite another. As the century draws to a close in this country we somehow find ourselves lumbered with both, and in the play I satirized this tendency by making my leading character a vicar who said he always distrusted priests who approached their parishioners 'usually with a lot of talk about Jesus – always a danger sign in my opinion'.

The experience of meeting these good souls left me confused, because although I liked them so much personally – liked them, I suspect, far more than I would ever like their fundamentalist brethren – it did seem to me, as an outsider, that they were perhaps overlooking some essential point about the Christian religion. If Christ did rise from the dead, then call me a fanatic, but I think you probably do have to tell people about it. The inner-city priest's conviction that the poor, for some reason, don't need to be brought up to speed on the news, does seem to be vaguely insulting. The Christian faith, after all, is based on the idea of intervention. Mankind is bowling along, following his own sinful ways, and then once and for all – for reasons which his Son then seeks to explain to us, but essentially because God has begun to despair of us – the physical rules of the universe are suspended and God intervenes. I cannot see how if the facts of Christ's life are true, they do not change everything.

It was here, with this most important point, that I began to confront the real implications of my presuming to write a play about the Church. I had embarked on it somewhat blithely, assuming that I broadly liked and admired these essentially decent people. To a degree, I thought them ridiculous, but certainly no more so than playwrights, or judges, for that matter. And overall, I wanted to put them before the public as examples of people whose way of life was genuinely valuable. Anyone who comes at the modern world from a different angle has my vote. I also admired G. K. Chesterton's remark that the Bible story is so unlikely that it must be true. Indeed, I regard that as more or less the most convincing defence of Christianity I have ever heard. But then I was disturbed to realize that I was coming to agree with Kierkegaard that Christianity cannot be a 'to some extent' religion. Either it is true or it is not.

But what is it? The more I worked, the more I came to feel that although you may want to believe that Christianity's message may be boiled down to something – however vague – to do with love and its operations in the world, its authority does have to depend on two central claims, which no amount of modernist wriggling can quite dispose of. Christians are people who believe, first, that a man was born of a virgin. And if you ask for a doctor's chitty to excuse you believing even that one, nobody however is going to let you off what I think we may insist is the Christian dealbreaker: that a corpse did walk out of a tomb. These two claims seem to me historically to have exerted such a powerful hold over the human imagination that you cannot simply dump them for jetsam at the end of the twentieth century. It is not just that they are part of the ship. Without them, I'm not sure you have any ship at all. More than that, it is positively dishonest to pretend that if you believe them, then you will not be forced totally to reconstruct the model of the universe which you carry in your head. Intervention is not just one idea like any other. It is a different order of idea.

I suppose what I am saying is that it took the writing of the play *Racing Demon* to make me realize just how profound my quarrel is with the defining myth of Christianity. There were times when I listened to the arguments then raging, for instance, over the question of the ordination of women, and I found I was instinctively against the idea, not on the usual misogynist grounds that Jesus weirdly omitted to designate them for the job, but because I realized that women were in fact the only people likely to bring the unwelcome injection of vitality which would actually keep the whole charade of Christian belief going into the next century. But at other times I felt myself softening, quite simply moved by the palpable sense of goodness that radiates in some churches. If the test of an organization is its ability to generate individual . acts of kindness, then this was a fine organization.

Those of you who have seen the play will know that I choose to start it with a prayer in which a vicar addresses God on the problematic question of His conspicuous absence from the world. Drawing God's attention to the desperate state of the inner city, the vicar remarks that, at one level, people are resigned to the fact of God's absence. They know that God is going to say nothing. They are used to it. However, after so many years of divine silence, the joke is beginning to wear thin. When God had said 'nothing', they didn't realize he did genuinely mean nothing at all. It is, he remarks, with a mildness characteristic of the Church of England 'just beginning to get some of us down'.

The play kicked off in this manner because it has always astonished me that Christians so often overlook one of the central facts about their God – namely that, in this life, He is nowhere either to be seen or to be heard.

What is also peculiar about God's silence – I would even call it eerie – is that biblically it is a fairly recent development. In his book *God: A Biography* the American academic Jack Miles points out that in the Old Testament God starts out as someone people can talk to. Or at least He is someone who talks to them. Throughout the early wanderings, the Jewish God is so often in conversation with individual humans that you could go as far as to call Him positively communicative. True, most of what He says is critical. In a paradox which I admit I have never wholly been able to grasp, God is forever communicating His displeasure with creation which has failed to come up to His expectation. He becomes, famously, the master of the rebuke and the lamentation. Yet after the Book of Job, He grows curiously more and more reticent. It is as if the sufferings of Job seem somehow to break his spirit and he speaks less and less. And in the whole of the New Testament, after sending His Son, He only says one thing, although it is something which even a non-believer finds extraordinarily beautiful: 'This is my beloved Son, in whom I am well pleased.' After this final statement, for the two thousand years which have followed, He is not on record as saying anything at all.

Given this defining feature of God's existence – that He will not, in any terms which you will recognize as being of this world, help you until the day you die with the question of whether He exists or not – then the surprise of those religious surveys which I mentioned at the beginning is not that so few people can articulate their spiritual beliefs but that anyone can at all. As a child, nothing put me off God more than my schoolteachers' highly selective habit of claiming to see Him in whatever suited them – be it in a daffodil or indeed in the abundance of nature. He was there, they said, in the stars. You could even tell He existed by watching the television programmes of David Attenborough. But the appropriation of everything which is good or beautiful or various as evidence of God always struck me even as a child as a particularly dishonest habit. 'When I look out across the fields and see the sun rising, then I know God exists' is a sentiment which has, throughout human history, engendered a quite terrifying quantity of poetry, both good and bad. Buckets of paint have been slapped on to canvas to make the same point. But when you think about it, it is an astonishingly feeble gambit. It can all too easily be countered by equally impressive arguments: 'When I look at a small child, buried at three with cancer, or when I contemplate that famous first charge in the Battle of the Somme, then I know He doesn't.'

For most of us, nothing is more off-putting in the Christian character than its *faux-naïf* habit of claiming everything which is conveniently positive and sliding over the things which are negative, or just consigning them to some marked-off philosophical dumping-ground called 'the problem of evil'. If everything which is good in the world is to be proffered and celebrated as evidence of God's existence, then what are we to make of the bad? After the recent massacre at Dunblane you were grateful for the fact that no honest churchman even attempted to answer the difficult questions. An agonised Dean of the Cathedral on the television that night made a deeply sincere impression when he admitted that it was impossible to provide any immediate reasoning which could make sense of what had happened, or which could offer any proper consolation to the bereaved. But I am sure the Church equally did itself considerable damage the next morning when it allowed some cocksure vicar on the *Today* programme to go on and piously assert that 'God has a special place for little children'. This kind of certainty – when we all know there is no certainty – is not just deeply offensive, it is perceived by the rest of us as being profoundly anti-humane. It remains for the parents of the murdered children, experiencing a torment which we cannot even begin to understand – and of which the radio vicar most certainly knows nothing – to decide where their children are now, if indeed they are anywhere. If we who do not believe take reasonable care not to trample on the religious feelings of those who profess them sincerely, then why can we honest doubters not ask an equal respect from churchpeople?

It is at moments like these when the Church does what one character in *Racing Demon* calls 'all that awful claiming you do' that some of us become positively hostile to the strategies of religion. For as long as Christian practice is, effectively, social work, we are grateful for it. Our gratitude has more than a whiff of bad conscience. You are willing to do work which we are not. You will spend time with the sick and grieve with the dying. You will try to heal the wounds which a class of ideological politicians has created in society at large. But when Christianity then goes on to the offensive and starts telling us that the suffering we endure here in this world is somehow justified, that it even has meaning because it is part of an absent God's larger plan and purpose, then we become angry. We are angry because we sense a certain unwelcome opportunism in religion which seeks to follow its own agenda and capitalize on our grief. We do not accept your view of the world as some sort of divine laboratory in which we are effectively rats, reacting or failing to react to religious stimuli. We do not wish to be told in St Paul's most disgusting metaphor – a metaphor indeed which reduces human beings even further, to the mere status of things – that we have no more right to criticize God than 'the clay has the right to criticize the potter'.

You will sense from what I am saying how hard I think it is to find any sense of proper proportion in a life dedicated to propagating the Gospel of Christ. Go too far in one direction, as perhaps my likeable friends in the inner city have done, and your tone becomes laughably apologetic. What Anglicanism's admirers would call its open-mindedness comes across all too easily as lack of fundamental conviction. The doctrine of turning the other cheek seems not just quixotic but downright disingenuous in the face of the modern world. But head off in the other direction and you pretty soon start to fall victim to practices which violate people's own sense of the privacy of their sufferings. Who, looking at the spectacle of millionaire preachers seeking out cancers among the elderly in California convention halls, or the equally grotesque money-driven antics at Lourdes, can doubt that Christianity is a religion whose power has traditionally depended in part on the almost unique ease with which it can be perverted?

After a while, I came to believe that this disturbing problem of tone, which hamstrings the modern Church and so easily sets one tendency against another, was not a coincidence, but instead actually told you something about Christianity itself. Like some other religions it has survived precisely because no one can quite say what it is. It was that devout Christian Dorothy Sayers who remarked of the Athanasian Creed that by the time it had informed you that God the Father was incomprehensible, Jesus Christ was incomprehensible, and the Holy Spirit was incomprehensible, you were perfectly justified in concluding that the whole thing was incomprehensible. But who can deny she had a point? So many of Christ's actions and sayings seem to me so deeply ambiguous and so prone to so many different interpretations and conflicting meanings – who for instance can ever understand why on earth He casually blasted that fig tree? What on earth was that about? – that it is hard to resist the conclusion that the durability of the religion bearing his name is down to the fact that it can stretch and bend in almost any direction you choose. (The fig tree, let's remember, was just standing there when He blasted it, and what's more, in just the sort of display of vulgar magic which otherwise He tells us He deliberately disdained.)

Of course it is true that all prophets depend on a certain inscrutability in order to achieve a desirable longevity. As a director friend of mine who longed to be compared to Peter Brook once remarked: 'I'd like to be a guru, but I can't do the silences.' Anyone like me who lived through the would-be student revolutions of the sixties is well used to the idea that the most influential prophets are always the ones whose precise meanings are hardest to discern. In those days, as soon as you said anything definite on the subject of, say, Karl Marx or indeed about Marxism itself, you would at once be told by some superior soul that you had insufficiently understood Marx. Or that your simplistic view of Marx did not take into account some factor or another. Or that if you could read him in the original German, you would know that of course he did not say what you thought he did. And of course there was always the most familiar excuse of all, and one which I think may even resonate on these sacred premises: that Marx was not a man whose ideas had been tried and found wanting, but – wait for it – a man whose ideas had never been tried.

However, even by the standards of other charismatic thinkers like Marx and Freud, Jesus Christ was prone to making comments which seem to support an almost infinite variety of exegesis. It was once said that by definition economists could not be expected to get anything right, because, of course, if they did, the world would only need one economist. In some sense, it is not up to a god to explain himself. That is left to the disciples. But a remark like 'Render therefore unto Caesar the things that are Caesar's, and unto God the things that are God's' could almost have been produced by computer scientists working at the cutting edge of linguistic theory to formulate . the single human sentence responsive to the greatest imaginable number of readings. No sooner does anyone tell you it is quite simple and that they know exactly what it means than someone else pops up to tell you it means the precise opposite. Anyone who heard Margaret Thatcher claim that the Good Samaritan was only empowered to do good because he had first worked hard to amass a considerable private fortune – naturally enough, as anyone who has read the story recalls, by the sweat of his own brow and, specifically, as St Luke is at pains to point out, without any debilitating Palestinian state subsidy – will know that the Bible often seems like some massive, incoherent natural resource, a kind of philosophical building skip full of old planks and plumbing, waiting to be looted for purely private purposes by any old madwoman with a handbag who happens to come along. No wonder it is the book which has traditionally provided so much inspiration to raving loonies in the street.

Is there anything firm, then, we may say about Christian teaching, which cannot be reasonably countered by someone anxious to swing the myth round to suit their own prejudices? Perhaps I am only confirming a few prejudices of my own, but I do not see how anyone claiming to look objectively at the bulk of the teachings can deny that this is an anti-materialist religion. At every stage Christ seems quite clear that our values should not be determined by our physical needs. What's more, Christ was incontestably a man who preached the idea that one day everything will be reversed. Whatever else He was, He was a man who liked the idea of re-ordering. He draws me in, as He does many people, when He propounds the initially attractive idea that eventually – in whichever world, this or the next one – the first shall be last and the last shall be first. It is a peculiarly satisfying prospect. Like everyone else, I become excited at the thought of that wonderful moment when we're all going to sit watching those rich bastards bloodying the sides of their camels in a desperate attempt to force them through the eyes of needles. One of the funniest sights I have ever seen on television was the ineffable Lord

Hailsham, after a lifetime of service to the interests of the rich, seeking to explain to us that Christ didn't really mean it when He said it would be hard for them to get into heaven. But oh yes He did. If Christ may be said to speak from anywhere at all, it is from a platform of redistributive justice. Here at least is one saying of Christ's which cannot be glossed out of existence. The meek, whoever they are, will one day inherit the earth.

But it is when we consider this possibility a little more closely that our doubts begin to creep in. It is those words 'one day' which stick in our throats. We are living after all in an age which has been uniquely disfigured by its appetite for violence. As Eric Hobsbawm points out in his history of this century, *The Age of Extremes*, it is sobering now to realize that the infamous pogroms which started the mass migration of Jews out of Russia at the end of the nineteenth century did not claim millions of victims. They did not even claim hundreds. The entire Diaspora, which rightly so shocked the Western world at the time, was triggered by the loss of only dozens of lives. To us, today, sickened and bloodied by the overwhelming statistics of mass murder in our own time, the numbers seem almost trifling.

Since the defining moment of our century, that moment when it became acceptable, even expected, to extend warfare into the civilian populations at home, we have seen an exponential growth in the number of innocent people who have been caught up in wars for which they have not volunteered. If we add together the best estimates we have for those killed in major conflicts this century – the First World War – ten million; the Russian Civil War – ten million; the Russians in the Second World War and after in Stalin's camps – twenty million; the Jews of Europe – six million; China in all wars – twenty million; the rest of us in the Second World War – fifteen million, et cetera – then we arrive at a community of the dead numbering one hundred and ten million. They have died by the violence we inflict on each other. In the shadow of this numbing, overwhelming horror, what meaning does it have to sit and pretend that one day, oh *one day* everything will be set right?

My own view is that Christianity is declining in the West because, in our hearts, many of us can no longer make any honest sense of it. Its essential message – which is that of justice delayed – seems simply too far off for it to have much impact on us. We have always, perhaps, had trouble with a God who seems to have set life as some sort of insane examination paper which, he tells you, you will pass or fail according to whether you do or do not choose to believe in his existence. But in a century which has been marked out by mass brutality on an unprecedented scale, by the rise of random terrorism, and by the persecution of particular racial and political groups to a degree which almost defies the imagination, it simply seems silly to go on worshipping a God who is represented as telling you that you will finally be rewarded or punished, according to whether you are or are not willing to accept the terrifying intangible evidence of His existence. It offends many people's most profound sense of what they feel life to be. Frankly, in the charnel house of the twentieth century, it scarcely matters. What matters is when and how the killing will stop.

In saying this, I have to make clear that I am not sure in my own mind whether Christianity has recovered from the ethical disaster of the Second World War. If it were true that religion has been simply powerless to prevent any of this rise in global suffering, then at least one might regard it as well meaning but irrelevant. But the evidence is all too plain that in some notorious cases, still unresolved, it has actively contributed to it. It is hard for us all once more to contemplate the behaviour of Pope Pius XII, but no one who has ever faced the real facts of how God's representative behaved in relation to the genocide inflicted by Hitler on the Jews can escape the uneasy conclusion that it throws some small light on dangers within Christianity itself.

Even Pope Pius's most passionate defenders will admit that he knew full well what was going on in the death-camps of Poland and Germany. He was apprised by independent witnesses, some of whom are still alive today, and who have testified to telling him directly of the scale and horror of what was going on. The decision he then made not to speak out against the massacres, and to advise his Cardinals to maintain a similar silence, remains, by any standard, the greatest blemish on the Christian religion in this century. When he might have warned his flock not to take part in their hideous work, he did not. As one honest German Catholic remarked, 'Each of us has to grope our own way, abandoned and alone.' Yet looking at what is plainly an act of moral madness, we can only understand it when we realize evil is always done by people who believe there is some cause more important than human decency. Here was a man whose actions can only make sense if we judge them by his own dismal criteria – did I save the Church? Did I preserve its power? – and who actually believed that these criteria should prevail over the ones which really mattered: did I sit in the Vatican and not lift a finger to prevent six million fellow human beings being needlessly slaughtered?

Pius XII's shocking story is that of a man who put the prosperity of his own Church above that of common humanity. For as long as he believed that the survival of his faith was more important than the survival of ordinary people, he was powerless to help human beings on earth. When he was told of the honourable Dutch Bishops who bravely took the other course and protested to the Germans, he became angry, even deliberately exaggerating the effects of their protests – ninety-two people died, not 40,000 as he pretended – in order to justify his own cowardice. By the most charitable interpretation one may say this was a man who had his priorities skewed. But by any humanist judgement, his 1942 Christmas message marks him as suffering from an evil, an evil in its way as corrosive as that which led to the murder of the Jews in the first place. What are we to make of a Pope who, in the only public reference to the camps in his whole life, could not even bring himself to utter the word 'Jew'?

One might think this a historical aberration of no consequence, no more important, say, than the Inquisition or any one of the religious wars which scarred the Middle Ages, simply the usual story of the wrong man in the wrong place. It might by now, with the passage of time, be thought to have no particular significance. But the disturbing fact is that it was the very intensity of this man's religious faith which led him into his terrible behaviour in the first place. The recent news that people in the Vatican are now lobbying to confer sainthood on the man who did most to discredit Christianity in our age makes you wonder if it is not endemic to this religion – or at least to this form of it – to put the need to prove you are right above the need to prove you are compassionate. At one level it is amusing that it takes four hundred years for a church to admit that it was in error when it broke the greatest genius of the Renaissance and destroyed his life. But at another level the problems Galileo had with organized religion have not gone away. When these same Cardinals tell gay men that they are in sin when they wear condoms, you are aware that a Church which funked the greatest moral crisis of the century, the extermination of the Jews, is now funking another, the spread of the new plague – and for exactly the same reasons. These are people who truly do believe that there are more important things on earth than our common humanity.

You may think it unfair of me to appear to implicate one church in the crimes of another. Be clear: that is not my intention. What Rome did cannot be Canterbury's fault. But I use this example – the most egregious piece of Christian behaviour in our time, and the aftermath of it – because it illustrates the very thing which worries me most about Christianity: that it almost necessarily encourages men and women to take their eye off the ball. No religious statement of the present day has moved me as much as the member of the million-strong congregation who shouted out spontaneously at the present Pope just as he raised the cup for a mass communion in the open air in Nicaragua: 'We asked for bread and you brought us stones.' Many Catholics, in good conscience, now have the integrity to ignore the worst of what comes out of the Vatican. But even so, for myself, I cannot get over the fact that they belong to a universal fellowship whose inevitable and, I think, fatal tendency is to have one eye on this life and one eye on a second. It is, I am afraid – and from this stems my fundamental distrust of it – an essential part of Christianity to believe that our aim is not towards this life, but towards another. I can only say, based purely on my own experience, that I do not believe this is a healthy way to live.

My position, self-evidently, is that of the agnostic. But I do not, like some agnostics, say 'We do not know'. I go further. I say 'We cannot know'. And given that we cannot know, we are faced with a choice. Which is more moral, which is more creative? To live as if we are only here once and make what sense of things we can? Or is it better practice to offset all the disappointments and pain of life by investing our hopes in some sort of eventual get-out, a moment at which the judgements we have made on earth will be reversed? Should we live for the moment when we see other meanings, other values behind the discernments we have made?

Of course, in asking this, I know that all the Christians I respect believe that their mission is in the here and now, and that they must have no expectation of any future. Over and again, they repeat that they must count on nothing for themselves. Nothing is guaranteed. The best Christians are the ones who work as if there is no tomorrow. But I still could not help observing in the months spent with my vicars that there is a subtle loss of urgency, a certain psychological softness in the way you approach life if you subscribe to a religion which teaches you that there is something else beside life itself. There is a moment at which your mind drifts upwards. Justice on this earth seems to matter less to you if justice will one day be delivered in another.

I suppose I cannot help believing agnostics live a life which is tougher and in some sense nobler than yours. Whatever your sincere mutterings about your own shortcomings, the fact is, all your money is not on this race. You have a side-bet, and that side-bet is with someone whose intentions you cannot hope to understand. For us, there is only one life. Judgement is here, either within ourselves or within the hearts of the people we love.

Therefore for us it is bitterly hard. Not for us the consolation of the famous joke, which I admit does amuse me, even though I know it to be wrong: 'Cheer up, life isn't everything.' We cannot go peacefully to our graves unless we feel at peace with what we have done here and here alone. To you, waste is a necessary fact of existence. It is written into the contract. For us, waste is sin. For you, everything will one day be put right. For us, we must work to make it right now. For you, the way you die scarcely matters for it will seem to be irrelevant under the eye of eternity. For us, eternity has no eye. How we die will be the test of our humanity.

I have spoken here today in the Abbey because, unlike those in what I have called the Christian fall-back position, I happen to think it a matter of great importance that we do work out exactly what we believe. It is time well spent. I have always had the instinct that even if it does not matter today, it may matter one day – and sooner than we think.

The most important fact of my life happened before I was born. In the Second World War millions of people died in defence of a belief, and the sense of squalor and disappointment of the post-war period seems to me inexorably to have stemmed from the feeling that the sacrifice they made has somehow been squandered. I mean no disrespect to Salman Rushdie when I say that his story in the last six years seems to me to be that of someone forced to decide whether they are, indeed, ready to die for their beliefs. When he was first put into a form of effective imprisonment, Salman was seen to thrash around like a man who could not actually believe that he might be killed for the principle of free speech. He issued contradictory statements, said things he later regretted, and generally behaved like someone who was being treated in a way which he found unfair. Yet as the years of captivity have gone on he appears to have found, through his own moral struggle, a form of acceptance – not, goodness knows, an acceptance that he is willing to die, but that if he dies, it will have been for a cause worth dying for. From the moment of that acceptance his stature has only grown. Which of us could have done better?

The one thing that remains to me to do in conclusion is to explain the title of this talk, 'When Shall We Live?' It is part of a pagan saying which – if I may pay an inverted compliment – seems to me to have a force which is almost Biblical. Some of you will know it. It comes from Seneca. Fond, as you might say, of his food and relishing the company of his friends and the prospect of the moments in front of him, he would sit down at table and ask a simple question, just before the dinner was served. This question – a form of grace, let's call it – rings with an historical urgency which is almost pre-Christian, and which one day in some unimaginable future may even justify that strange word 'post-Christian'. Looking at the feast in front of him, Seneca liked to observe: 'When shall we live, if not now?'